HANDFAST

Poetry Duets

by

Ruth Aylett

&

Beth McDonough

Mother's Milk Books

First published in Great Britain in 2016 by Mother's Milk Books

ISBN 978-0-9954516-1-2

Typeset in Georgia, Old Newspaper Types and Squares by Teika Bellamy. Old Newspaper Types font designed by Manfred Klein. Squares font designed by Listemageren.

Printed and bound in Great Britain by The Russell Press, Nottingham, on FSC paper and board sourced from sustainable forests.

www.russellpress.com

First published in 2016 by Mother's Milk Books
www.mothersmilkbooks.com

CONTENTS

A litany across generations

Running beside her racing words
I try to match speeds, jump into her
timeline, grasp the 'him', the 'theirs' — sweet
kernels in these memory beads her fingers
comfort tell, solid in the past. If
I'm your daughter not your mother, we are
now not then — but where's the point
in shouting truths that only hurt the heart?

Anyway, who owns this heart — this bright
million-shattered glass? Whose heart? I know
we shared a body once, pulsed our blood in time,
rhythmed all those months, but now
we struggle as we sequence words,
to find some safer place to put
our truths, work out clearer ways to fit
a future both of us can bear to hold.

You string your cared-for beads of almost words,
I nearly hear swirl sounds, clack-mouthed,
sensed like wombfuls, rhythmic kinds of chora.
We keen to share a code but speech
over-patterns you, my semaphore just clouds —
all closed-in metaphors, dark with phrased excludes.
It's good for you, I say. You know it's not.
I polish the lie at my throat.

And who owns the lies that lie between
us? Spilled in a needling tangled hedge,
spear-sharps outwards, blocking, set to lacerate
my gentling hand into screamed frustration;
taking out my eyes, to see only the prickle
swirl of deadened lights against
the eyelids — you, the darkness radiating
on wavelengths beyond my sight.

Sightless now, I spin on all this clatterspill,
try to still, pick and thread these beads,
seek a motif, find reasoned patterns;
fumble for some catch that could exist,
then loop this line across my fingers, throat
where touch might finally decode
the hissing crackle of your inmost space,
unfold the map we need to bring us home.

Days in the life

Young doctor, wild medic celebration,
war's-end, pure alcohol punch party-framed

Escaping post-war greyness, French hay truck
high-riding southwards, honeymoon joy-framed

Anxious elderly primagravida
knowing too much groans 'push-now', baby-framed

Sinuous Morrison, Liberty prints,
skirts, curtains, busy sewing-machine framed

Food adventures garlic mussels ginger
impressionistic herb-scatter framed

Sixties suddenly free Tamla dancing
op-art dresses, wine, dinner-party framed

Doctor surface, calm cool, examining,
drug dependency clinic career-framed

After-dinner port, ladies rise to leave
refusnik sitting tight, equal-rights framed

Daughter demonstrator: see this is how,
wave balance, me you us all, future-framed

No such thing as the wrong kind of weather photographs…

Seurat scatters colour from birks in the park's frame
you cut out in camouflage tops, brilliant already dark frames.

Crab apples necklace by quince, drip to your trampoline
slipper slipped-off, you pyjama flip, bounce. Star-framed.

Kicked at the Ben's frosty skin, puddles crack
you brave up in boots, skliff cagoules, rucksack-framed.

Thicked in snow blotting, you angel out
fat salopette shape, all down. Christmas card framed.

Piney in March-sharpen woods, shared with Schiehallion
you are fleecewarm, flare-cheeks   run out of the far frame

Sunflashed, you jump shush pebble waves
rash vest, squint-shorts, cast hat. Haar framed.

Fallen from pier walls, scooped up by boats
you are soaked clothes, rush home, arm-framed.

Mud-shirted, twitched all through your left side
hospital wired. You are wee in that bed, metal-framed.

You silk unseasonal into your feel finest t-shirts, smirk at Mum's fuss.
Son, you tousle from clothes and from mantels, always charm-framed.

Equinoctial Stranger

Broken early, you wash from rough waters
vernixed
into this shaded world
in waken alive hope, in dreams
     beyond sixteen hours induced in this speckle wall rip-bordered room
of spillbowl cereal after school, of necked milk filched from the fridge
     after three paced shifts, tickleTENS relief countless counted huffs
of tumble first words, of curl back feet at the first feel of sea
     bleeped big heart bleeped wee heart bleep bleep
of ripped t-shirt, flayed knees, of four outrageous leaps from apple trees
     after bleed on bleed, shot on shot of Anti-D, Rhesus disease fears
of mank, floor-trips of Thomas the Tank Engine, of lego-sore prints on so
dinosaur squalls, dolls
     after all your older siblings had left, soon past the blue line
of scared out far too late, drunk, don't give a stuff, Mum
of snowswirls, lit lanterns, of mouthstains of bramble jam
of tongue out madpals at windowpanes sticky with 99 melts
of roll over hunkers through bracken down bens
of learning to lace up round pencil-shaped cases
of drawing, of blob pots, of hormones, of spots
of five pounds fifteen ounces
couried in   of hope.

Eclipse, 1999

Le Havre, a house-swap flat
under the path of the totality.
I drive you from Deauville
across the Pont du Normandie,
you hold onto the dash
and tell me again
the French do all this better.

Buying food is an issue.
Rice cakes with pureed tomatoes
no gluten no onions, cocoa
made with water not milk.
Though you still love mussels;
that night we all eat out.
I see the first shadow.

It gets dark gradually, the sun
shuttered by the black edge,
birds fly home to roost
conversation leaches out
into a silence. The dark centre
is sudden, a great over-flying.
Now, we remember.

Undoing tacking

Stubbornly *in situ* as you let go bit by bit
and lost your love of earrings, books;
you stopped cooking or watering the plants,
slept until midday, wandered at night,
drinking tea, afraid you might die in the dark.

Learning from your mistake
I moved to a ground floor flat
before legs, heart or brain went;
spent the summer packing and unpacking,
forcing furnishings into smaller rooms.

Those huge floor cushions covered with leafy
Morris fabrics, you gave me thirty years since.
How you embraced sixties home design
and big gestures, always generous. Covers
shabby, unwashed since my move before last.

Removing cover from cushion to clean
I slowly unpick the tacked closed end, each of your
stitches taken out drawing behind it the memory
of your last days. Letting you back in, young,
elegant, intent at your sewing machine.

To unravel a gansey

I never knitted you up, big-needled
with Calder hips (Mum and I kept *those*).
You raglaned out into your Dad's shape —
brave shoulders, neat form. In infancy, purled
between us, I caught his style across you,
your head a fuzzy angora buzz
with his mother's strawberry hair
her Celtic freckle pale skin.
My own Dad's triangle eyes and mine — snell
Buchan sea blue — loop
back. Friends pick up stitches, catch
expressions, pull threads. I try
not to rattledown patterns, tease
awkward gaps in fraternal chat.
Why twist in aspects of our family's allsorts, pick up
engineer geekiness, wired in the other side?
So many strands to unravel.
What could I ever make new
from all that telephoned wool?

What your garden grew

Hassle by dangle Granny Mutch bonnets, bruise
ginger mint, sage. Haul
impossible deep-thrall
bishop weed, then

let go. Steal by Jacob's ladders; find
lichen rungs damp
among lupin star leaves.

Hide up high, where a child once
limbed to some together place
in this red dark tree. Feel planks
loosen, settle as that unravel rope swing
rots greener, as the worm-door
playhouse sleeks off
a cheek of field mice. Tell yourself that blurry sheen
on the broken chute is
smirr
only smirr.

Cuttings

Gardening before garden centres,
his summer's end meant brown
paper bags rattling with seeds.

He made swaps, took cuttings
old wood or new, depending,
pushed into damp autumn earth.

He'd always save pods of
broad beans for the next crop,
set old potatoes to sprout in the dark.

His daughter left for the city
without a twig or growing tip
to plant, searched for years

for the unnamed yellow rose
climbing her grandmother's house;
consulted endless catalogues,

whatever she bought never quite right.
Shopped for clothes extravagantly,
released from sewing her own,

but visited famous gardens
with secateurs in her bag,
to appropriate their history.

The oleander she once gave me
now twenty years grown,
my own cutting: just rooted.

Hands

She was a doctor,
boxes of latex gloves.
She was a doctor.
'Where is my handbag?
I need to go to the toilet.'

Hands always cold,
removing a splinter
a blackened needle
sterilised red-hot with a match.

Hands that examined,
pressing swollen glands
'Open your mouth, say aaah.
You'd better stay in bed.'

She was a doctor,
a handbag of latex gloves.
She was a doctor,
'I practice self-evacuation,
need to go to the toilet.'

Gripped

You rough my arm, both hands
habit calloused. *He's grovin* — cat-scratching;
Gran's Doric curls

around actions she can't
understand — this
touch-insensitive touch.

Your fingers forage, find solace
in ripping grass, in slacked wrack,
in mud. You earth.

Frustration bites still oval
backhanded in scars, as your nails
crescent red into wrists. Your

fingers pull tight at the flip
clipper threat. Babyfists
muscled to manhood grip mine.

April wanderings

Out perhaps too late
for sense, mist milks out
spruced heights, erases
the Sidlaws with sharp
other worlds beyond. If
ticks and faeries air
we never ask. Just two
raucous pheasants rare this still.

We trust seeing feet
on knitted roots, pass wired-up
blaeberries, scratching in ling
on the bounce surprise of dry peat.

I shake last night's trek
in twigs from your shoes,
fit them, strap in your feet. You laugh
when I Lynx your teenage pits, fit
for this morning's new walk.

Midnight hour

When you woke
the day had turned
dark as midnight
uncurtained windows
glaring blackly in
and everyone had gone,
your son never
back from his football,
nor your parents
from their walk
and out on the street
someone had turned
the streetlights on
morphed the houses
into strangeness
the whole town gone
and you cold in your
nightie and slippers
and your front door
locked against you
and the key gone,
and the police
when they finally came
strangely gentle.

What am I?

My first is in distance
But absent from place
My second's in echo
And empty and space
My third's in my mind
But never right now
My fourth's in escaping
But found with a frown
My next is in nothing
And nowhere and none
My sixth's in the terror
Of meaning that's gone
My seventh is all
That it means to be me
My last is my first
And my last memory.

A regular riddle

I suspect you'd style me   a skinny type
yet that first year I knew myself   unique.
Very much the focus. Fêted,   in fact. They
ringed me, roused me   really lit me up —
all smiles   all songs.
He watched as I wavered, but   he *did* watch me.

Only a year on   my double dug her heel in
and after that   another. Every time — same attitude.

We surfaced, stuck it out.   Our stalky crew —
on frosted white, on flat,   on his face of late —
oh, he was always   there. Officially. Wide-eyed, upset
hands on head   hating that song, all that

annual admiration. He didn't give   a shit.

They burnt us down, begged him   *begged* him to save us.
He walked away.   Would not. Would not.

You know my name.   Now, his own riddle
may trouble you, and take   more time to solve.

Birthday postings

Through a baffle pillow
an early traffic boom bruises
into this wantless day. I turn
another ear, backache
into dawn. Yesterday's yarns
spool out. Later I steal

his trampoline-happy image, crop
his seventeen years of age-
inappropriate self
into that half-turn, great unaware smile.

I thread round his bolt from the car door,
his repeat pattern stalk in and away from
this party, pizza to toilet and back,
all unravelled presents, his never never want
to be there.

I filigree something round this day's holes
as Gran crocheted doilies
to save tables from vases. I silk him
beautiful onto the Facebook page
he'll never know
accept all the likes of our day.

Birthday

A day of sun and cloud
The same question again
and again 'Is it *my* birthday?
Who will come?'
'Who would you like?' we say.
Clouds deepening, looks like rain.

You invite the pharmacist
from your first ever job
the man who'd just lost his wife
and shouted at you so much
you dropped the jar
he'd asked you to fetch.

You invite all those young men
Canadian bomber pilots
birds of paradise in
workaday Somerset
they were so soon gone,
nothing but grief to love.

And the Indian officer who
bought you wonderful cloth
printed with scenes of France.
Your mother told you off
forbade you to write
now you'll be able to apologise.

A shower clatters on the window,
candle flames on your cake flicker
in the breath of your absent guests.
Uninvited but here, there's us.
And when you see your two sons
that brilliant smile reaches your eyes.

Waterworld

Is this a well where I find you
somewhere at the bottom?
It's dark down here and you
are the echo to my questions.

Are you dissolving in the bath
scented with rosemary?
Brain soft, crinkled as finger-tips,
dissociating into atoms?

Standing under the shower
my head up, eyes shut
light flares at each drop's impact,
my darkness glows with your shape.

His autism in the power of rain

We cowered to the kitchen from the rainthreat.
As a glowered sky grumbled on Angus, we
cosied, cupped our comfort of tea, bit buttered scones.
        Heaven ripped. We lost him.

Lost him for a million terrifies of seconds —

found him. Found him out in that Kirrie garden, danced
by the hard rain, stung-skinned on his seven year
naked of self, drenched in the joy of storms,
laughed happy. Wild in flashed lightning, he spun

joys our dried-out flesh still missed.

In Paris, without autism

She's wee, and almost lost in awe,
structured in the splendour of the Louvre
[God, he'd hate it here]
then she's wandered
mazy-wondered on Rive Gauche
[he'd run off here, get lost. He'd spin to find a hill].

Next day's cafe breakfast flakes
great croissants on her tights
[he likes them — told her so at three years old
in Corsica. Wanted nice. He pointed
then. Replaced his spoon. Ate].
She sharps in new pressed orange juice
[he can't bear bits in drinks. Have to find a sink.
Pour it all away].

This Metro fills
with straight out stares,
from worn street smarts
in city-smoggy skins [she scans
to find a nook for him, worries how he's
fascinated by the doors — fucksake, he's
in another country. He's fine. Sure. He's absolutely fine].

At Sacre Coeur, at Notre Dame, she can't
face all those confessionals glassed-in, that unkind
of public worship, can't light a candle, say
any prayer. Whose heart? What Lady? [whoop. Whoop.
New acoustics. Good]. Can't. Can't.

Modern art

You are leaving your own likeness very slowly,
a photograph bleached in years of sun,
colour and detail leaching out, only
crude brushstrokes and outlines remain,
a woman in Picasso distortion.

So I become a mourner by degrees:
ash on the face a finger dab at a time
one more strand of hair ripped from the scalp
each month; nail scratching across the face
as slowly as weathering fissures.

And the child wails forever that life
is just not fair, that some bad person
has abstracted her mother and left
this silent husk with empty eyes instead.
Can you smile now if you're still there?

Duty of care

For you, sleep never knitted ravelled sleeves,
you'd wander in and out of darkened rooms,
avoid the little death through brewing tea
then sleep from dawn until your lunch was due.

That nightly fear created in your head
a voice that told you never to lie down;
you slept in chairs, developed swollen legs
bruised sausages with ulcerated skin.

We call an ambulance when you get worse,
you tell the paramedics you're okay
in something like your former doctor's voice,
we contradict you, scared you'll fade away.

They lay you flat, you fight with piercing screams
that label us betrayers as you leave.

Michaelmas nights

We turntake scurries, 3 a.m
urgencies. Wait.Wait. Until one wall
away, we knot into wizen sheets — try
to dream-riddle possible days
haared in belief,
pegged out on the Tay. We charm
saucer nasturtium leaves, washed
in dawn's rainbows. Apple trees damp
hairstfull of chuffed pigeons.

Twisted through blood moons, we rope
dark shifts, bound by your shout-
tics. All of us spiral, rhythmed beyond
your sometime lost reason for rest. Our shins scuff
turn, tap, thread into this dark. We sore
for sleep's quench, ask to drown
into bramble torn lands
ready to scratch
that first one to fall.

On Diet and Autism

Of course, he will eat
an abnormally limited number of foods
alioli: baklava: chickpeas: dolmades

possibly only white meals —
potatoes, cauliflower and lemon sole
elderberry juice: fajitas: granola: hummus

Conceivably, he will insist
on a single flavour of just one brand of crisps
Indonesian rooty vegetable stew: Jaipuri chutney: Kalamati olives

No! Let's stop right here,
before we reach zucchini buds.
He eats everything I can —

but Dietician, what I don't know
is just how *many* olives.
He never leaves the stones.

Feeding frenzy

Self-diagnosing the aching gut
and distended abdomen
as lactose intolerance, she ate
rice biscuits, avoided dairy,
until her spine began to crumble
into unremitting pain, the world
repelled as much as gripped;
withdrew into silence though
occasionally that glorious smile
would still emerge, for the new
grandchild or her sons.

He packed a box each day
for hospital visits, tempted
her with strawberries, smoked salmon,
their sixties luxuries
from before farmed fish
and Spanish poly tunnels; brought
surreptitious ruby port
in an empty pickle jar.

Near the end the yoghurt drinks
were all she'd take because
he insisted these were medicine;
we smelt an acetone stink
close up as the body carried on
as best it could by feeding on itself.
'Dry' was almost the last thing she said.
Died as a dried husk, in her own bed.

Legacy

You planted this bamboo:
went all the way to Andûze,
and bought three different sorts;
'It will make a screen,' you said.
But installed in good black soil
enriched by river floods
the bamboo rioted and spread.

Now more thicket than screen
growing three metres tall
with large papyrus-like leaves,
and underground cables, iron-hard,
on which I broke a spade
after they invaded the lawn,
as a bamboo advance-guard.

You always gardened for wildness:
trees near the house grew too big,
shrubs into an impressionist embrace.
Hard to imagine so far ahead
how much it would all grow. Now
I'm digging out rampant bamboo
and you're in the ground, dead.

Preserving

I chank berried menisci together on sills
corner cloth spills set on necks.
Waxed discs drop
to pinkie on garnet. Soon
damp plasticed jam
is elastic-secure
vaccum-protected.

Those shrunk mirror tops watch
batterdown crows
shower in from boortrees.
Landing calm, they strut
their ancestors' grounds. As they hunt
for unknowns, I can rob
no more tricks from my store.

What
can I give
to keep you always
safer than this?

Handfast

Where's the darning needle that can catch, up-loop
dropped stitches: a word undone, another moment gone

    Backwards chain 'Mum's very…'   Mum's very… Mum's   very…
    very
    Sometimes Mum's   happy.   Sometimes she's   fat.

    We adopt his literal phrasing, admire
    his unaware two finger wave at convention.

Again again again the best pupil in all Monmouthshire
asked by the hungry of the class for her apple core

Time-shifted night-walking tea-making
day-light bedclothes over head hidden

    Arms parcel your hoodie-covered face. We ask, tease,
    boo you into our world. You focus way beyond.

Our fear of your fear that summer hospital visiting time
returning from your past — I am dying — accusing us

    My biggest fear was where we three are now.
    Now? I fear for him when we *won't* be.

Lifting your arms so I can pull your nightie on
your head bends to the brush, hair so white, long

    When he holds me, trusts, loves, he has no
    artifice, no walls, nothing of that cold they suppose.

Our fingers cling-grip your unresponding skin
and try to Gulliver-tie you into living on

Puce mouth. Spit-edge. That tremble. Shake.
Irises gone. We can only hold. Time this. Speak. Hope.

About the Poets

Ruth Aylett lives in Edinburgh where she teaches and researches university-level computing, thinks another world is possible and that the one we have is due some changes. She was joint author of the collaborative online epic *Granite University* and performed with Sarah the Poetic Robot at the 2012 Edinburgh Free Fringe. She has been published by Envoi, Bloodaxe Books, Poetry Scotland, Red Squirrel Press, Doire Press and others. For more on her writing see: www.macs.hw.ac.uk/~ruth/writing.html

Beth McDonough trained in silversmithing at Glasgow School of Art, and has taught art in a variety of sectors. Many years later she returned to Dundee University to complete an M.Litt. She continues to work between disciplines. Her reviews are published regularly by *DURA*, where she is poetry editor. She is on the editorial team at *The Fat Damsel* and at *The Poets' Republic*. Writer in Residence at Dundee Contemporary Arts (2014–16), she is part of the interdisciplinary Tay Clay Project and a contributor to *New Boots and Pantisocracies* and *Scotia Extremis*. Her poetry may be read in *Gutter*, *The Lighthouse*, *The Interpreter's House*, *Northwords Now*, *Antiphon* and many other places.

She finds poems riddling with Anglo-Saxons, foraging and swimming in cold waters. She thanks Jim Stewart and Kirsty Gunn of Dundee University and her fellow poets locally for their supportive criticism. Her gratitude is also due to her husband and Ochil Tower School (Camphill Scotland). Together with her son, they have all made *Handfast* possible.

An earlier version of 'His autism in the power of rain' was published online at *Rainy Fiction* (April 2014). 'On Diet and Autism' first appeared in *Southlight 17* (April 2015). 'A litany across generations' was placed second in Cheltenham Poetry Festival's Compound Poem competition 2015.

Mother's Milk Books
is an independent press, founded and managed by
at-home mother, Dr Teika Bellamy.

The aim of the press is to celebrate femininity
and empathy through images and words,
with a view to normalizing breastfeeding.
The annual Mother's Milk Books Writing Prize, which
welcomes poetry and prose from both adults and children,
runs from September to mid-January.
Mother's Milk Books also produces and sells art
and poetry prints, as well as greetings cards.
For more information about the press, and to make purchases
from the online store,
please visit: www.mothersmilkbooks.com